For my parenting partner,

Lets be on the
"cutting edge" of
parenting.

With love

THE RETRONAUT GUIDE TO
RAISING CHILDREN

THE RETRONAUT GUIDE TO

RAISING CHILDREN

WOLFGANG WILD

ilex

An Hachette UK Company
www.hachette.co.uk

First published in the UK in 2016 by ILEX, a division of Octopus Publishing Group Ltd
Carmelite House, 50 Victoria Embankment, London, EC4Y 0DZ
www.octopusbooks.co.uk

Design, layout, and text copyright
© Octopus Publishing Group 2016

Distributed in the US by Hachette Book Group
1290 Avenue of the Americas, 4th and 5th Floors, New York, NY 10020
Distributed in Canada by Canadian Manda Group
664 Annete St., Toronto, Ontario, Canada M6S 2C8

Publisher: **Roly Allen**
Commissioning Editor: **Zara Larcombe**
Managing Specialist Editor: **Frank Gallaugher**
Senior Project Editor: **Natalia Price-Cabrera**
Editor: **Rachel Silverlight**
Art Director: **Julie Weir**
Designer: **Tina Smith**
Assistant Production Manager: **Lucy Carter**

ISBN 978-1-78157-300-6

A CIP catalogue record for this book is available from the British Library
Printed in China

CONTENTS

INTRODUCTION

Retronaut—the past like you wouldn't believe—is all about tearing little holes in your map of time. Here's how it works. You and I are walking around in the world, each with a map of the past in our heads. Our maps have been assembled from the sum total of every picture, every film, every sound, every song and every story of the past that we have encountered across our lives. Our minds stitch all these pieces together into our mental maps of time, and we each call our own map "the past."

Your map and my map are different—we each have memories that the other doesn't. And events that loom large on my map may not feature on yours at all—and vice versa. Some events, though, are obvious features on both our maps—like the Millennium, 9/11, and the two World Wars. But here's the thing. They are foggy, blurred, indistinct. Some parts of our maps are very detailed indeed, others have almost no detail at all. We use single words to sum up entire decades—the "Swinging" Sixties, the "Roaring" Twenties. And, by and large, our maps are in black and white. Because so many of the photographs we have seen of the past are black and white, even though logically we know the past was full of color, our maps are mainly in monochrome. Not only that, the people on our maps are walking very fast, just as they do in early films. And the people are either silent, or they speak in tiny, tinny voices.

The result is that when we imagine the past, it's often as something sepia, stiff, dusty—and

dead. And that's where Retronaut comes in. Retronaut knows that "the past" as something different from the present, different from this moment, from "now"—this past—does not exist. The past was, and is, all part of a very long "now." There is no division between "now" and "then." And no one has ever lived in "the past"—they have only ever lived in "now," but it was a different version. And so, Retronaut is dedicated to hunting down pictures, film, sound, stories and songs that don't feature on our maps. That do not seem like the past at all. That tear tiny holes in our mental maps of time. We want to show that, in the words of William Faulkner: "the past is never dead. It is not even past."

Retronaut came about because ever since I was a child, I have wanted to do one thing—go back in time. As a boy, I was fascinated by the wonder of the past. It seemed to me to be as exotic as another country—but one I could never visit. That seemed to me to be a shame, to say the least. Almost a design flaw in the

AS A BOY, I WAS FASCINATED BY THE WONDER OF THE PAST. IT SEEMED TO ME TO BE AS EXOTIC AS ANOTHER COUNTRY— BUT ONE I COULD NEVER VISIT.

universe. And so I fell in love with children's stories of time-travel, of people who discovered a secret door that led them back into times gone. I looked and looked for my secret door, but never found it. Wanting to go back in time is not an obvious career choice, and so I buried my desire for years, decades, until it was reawakened when I discovered a book of color photographs from the 1940s. These color pictures were of the past, but they didn't look like the past at all—they were not sepia, stiff, dusty or dead. They looked just like "now." The color dissolved away the distance, like polish dissolving tarnish on a ring.

These old color photographs were my door. For the next few years, walking through my door became my passion. I avidly collected as many color pictures of the past as I could, finding them in second-hand book shops and charity shops—though rarely online. Soon, I found other doors as well as early color photography. I realized that all I had to look out for was something—anything—that didn't fit with the way I imagined the past, that didn't belong on my mental map. Find that, and I would have given myself a time-travel hit. This is how I got that hit. For a moment, I would do a mental double-take. My head would be temporally dislocated. "That can't be from the year it says it's from!" I would think. "What's happened? Either I have traveled in time, or the way I imagine that year is wrong." Then there would be a pause, and then I would have to change the way I imagined that point in time. The material had made a hole in my map of the past.

For many years, I collected all the photographs I found—and the sounds, and the videos, and the illustrations—on my Mac. Then, one day in the Autumn of 2009, I met a friend of mine, John, in a Lebanese cafe in Paddington, London. I was showing John the collection on my computer. "You should start a blog," he said…Knowing nothing about blogging, I googled "What to call your blog." It seemed that "How to…" was a good start—how to bath your dog, how to make your lawn greener etc. Well, I wanted to show people how they could go back in time—or at least feel like they had, even just for a nano-second. But "How to go back in time" didn't seem quite cool enough. What was a word for someone who went back? Like an astronaut, but only going backwards? A "retronaut."

And so I started my shiny new blog at the beginning of January 2010. I loved creating it, and adding to it. It also gave me a chance to do something that I had always wanted to do, but never had the opportunity to do before—to curate. I am not a trained curator, nor ever likely to be, and a professional curator is a highly specialized job. But to be able to choose, show, and share pictures in the way I wanted to was deeply satisfying. In a very small way, I was a curator. For three weeks the audience for Retronaut was approximately two—my mother and I. And between us we amassed around 200 hits a day. Then, one day, at the end of January, one of the posts went viral, and ended up on

IN THIS BOOK, YOU WILL FIND EXTRAORDINARY IMAGES OF CHILDREN SMOKING. CHILDREN RIDING IMPROBABLE ANIMALS. CHILDREN USING UNBELIEVABLE TECHNOLOGY.

the front page of *Reddit*. The post was a set of color high-resolution Kodachrome pictures of central London in 1949, taken by the beautifully named Chalmers Butterfield. People would look at these gorgeous, super-colorful, super-resolution shots. "Cool pictures," they would say. "Is that a film-set? It can't be, it's too real. But it looks like a digital picture—and it's in color. I didn't think they even had color in 1949!" And then their mind would do the double-take, the hole in their map of the past was torn. And then they would share the pictures with their friends.

The result for me was 30,000 hits in one day. And the rest is history. Or rather, Retronaut. The underlying message of Retronaut is that what may seem to us today to be fixed, essential, and inevitable, may simply be another version of now. It's a message of freedom and potential. Nothing is fixed, everything can be changed, remixed, recurated. And that includes ourselves.

For this book, we have chosen to focus on the subject of children. More than most subjects we explore on Retronaut, children resonate with almost of us, because, hey, we've all been children, right? (Maybe we still are). But this can blind us to the sometimes quite extraordinary changes over the last hundred years in the ways we have perceived children in the past. In this book, you will find extraordinary images of children smoking. Children riding improbable animals. Children using unbelievable technology. Children attached to the most unwieldy of contraptions. Children hanging out and hung up, and hanging others up. Children who look like adults. Children who look desperately in need of an adult. Children inside impossibly small things. Children playing with impossibly big things. Children afraid of the familiar. Children that terrify. Children seemingly in grave peril. And children putting people in grave peril. And children with more and stranger weapons than you might think wise.

What every photograph has in common is that we believe it will show you a picture of children of the past like you wouldn't believe. Each one is evidence that our understanding of childhood, that most basic building block of what it is to be human, has been ever in flux. It's absolutely not fixed. Because, actually, nothing is fixed. Everything is capable of change. Including you.

Wolfgang Wild, author

1900: A mother and father transport their child.

1890: A mother and father tow their child on a tandem Pennyfarthing.

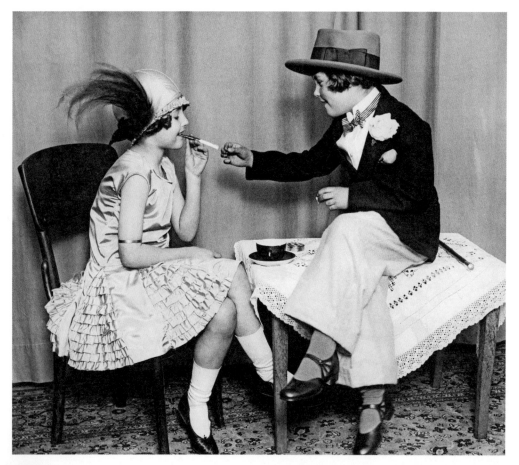

1928: Two girls pose as a man and a woman. Location not known.

1930s: In New York, two children examine their dolls with a stethoscope.

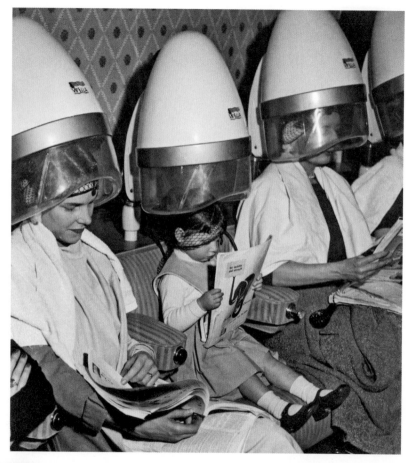

1957: Three-year-old Jaqueline Power of Maida Vale, London having a shampoo and set for the Christmas party season.

c. 1950: A girl occupies herself reading while her dolls have a perm at a Viennese barber.

c. 1930: At a Los Angeles air show, a little girl sits on a trophy holding two model aeroplanes.

RIGHT **1931:** The son of a glider pilot demonstrates a working model of a seaplane, England.

LEFT C. **1936:**
Children in costume
representing chess
pieces stand on a
giant chess board
during a chess week
in England.

1934: Children
playing a giant game
of draughts or
checkers in a park in
Tottenham, London.

c. 1950s: Two boys take to a makeshift boxing ring.

RIGHT **Early 1900s:** A postcard of two very young boys boxing as a man and a woman in evening dress look on. The child on the far right is checking his watch, possibly timing the round.

1964: A young boy playing on the pebble beach at Brighton with a miniature earth-moving machine, one of the latest mechanical toys then on show at the 11th British Toy Fair.

1964: A boy sits in a model of a 1919 bus at the finish line of the London-to-Brighton vehicle run.

1941: Two Russian kindergarten children wearing paper butterflies for a game in which they pretend to fly.

RIGHT **Early 1900s:** Two little girls pose in a garden wearing matching costumes.

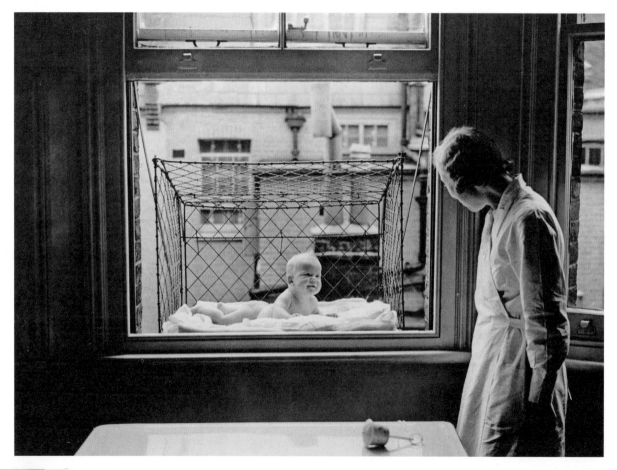

LEFT **c. 1937:**
A baby outside a
window in England,
in order to benefit
from fresh air.

1937: A small boy
left in a waste paper
bin in a London park,
while his brothers
play nearby.

1887: A little girl improvises a camera from a flowerpot and a stool to "photograph" her friend.

1934: The French photographer Robert Doisneau captures a little girl playfully blocking the lens of a fellow photographer.

LEFT **1930:** Two children play with different sizes of model Citroen cars as publicity for a Citroen dealership in Berlin.

1930: A Little girl surrounded by toy cars in a large Berlin toy store.

1954: A young boy takes aim while hiding in a coal hole.

RIGHT **1925:** A brother and sister pretend to paddle a Native American canoe with their toys, in a family photograph taken in England.

1972: Children jump from a bridge just as a freight train crosses a reservoir in Canada.

1944: A child plays on the beach at Bournemouth, England.

1930: A clown during a visit by the circus to a children's hospital in the USA.

1964: Father Christmas at a party in aid of the "Save the Children" Fund.

1955: Paul Carpenter training his 15-month-old daughter Ramona as an acrobat, South Gate, California.

1935: A grandfather plays with his granddaughter in Los Angeles.

1923: Child star Frankie Darro and his father practice stunts on the beach. Location not known.

c. 1926: Four-year-old Bernardine Blackburn with her father in Los Angeles, California.

c. 1930: Boys learning to swim at a school in Cincinnati, Ohio, USA.

RIGHT **1930s:** Two six-year-old boys playing draughts at the bottom of a pool in Winter Haven, Florida, USA.

LEFT **c. 1983:** Jason Dallaire, 11, a regular arcade goer, tries his skill against the video game Krull. Location not known.

1972: Two children using the ODYSSEY video game console. Location not known.

1940: Children play in a London nursery school playground.

1940s: An eight-
and nine-year-old girl
and boy playing in
the street. Location
not known.

LEFT **1939:**
Women and children
demonstrating a
range of adult and
child gas masks.

1963: A view of
a future where
industrial air
pollution makes
the wearing of a gas
mask a necessity
when going outside.

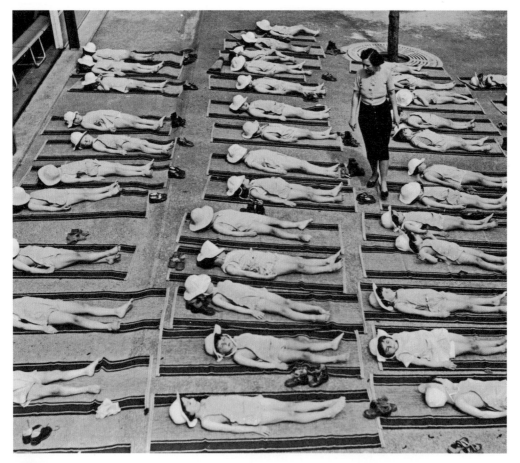

1939: Pupils at a progressive open-air school near Paris enjoy the sunshine.

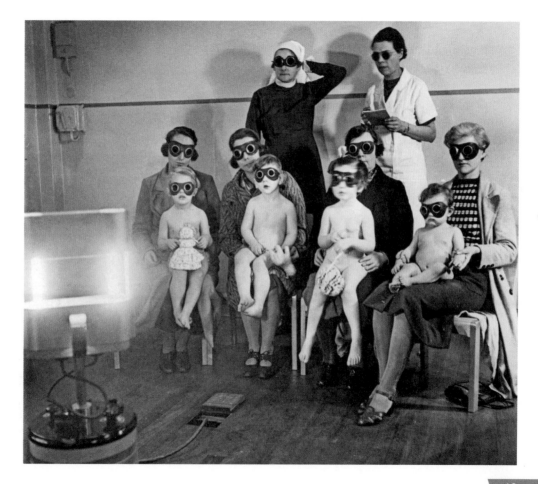

1938: Children receiving ray treatment at a Child Welfare Centre in London.

1939: Babies brought out for some sun by their nurses in Manchester, England.

RIGHT **1929:** Children sleeping on the roof of a British orphanage.

1903: A Rancher's daughter sitting in his prize-winning pumpkin. Location not known.

c. 1890: A boy seated on a chair on a table. Location not known.

1943: Young girls play with their dolls in the street in front of their house in Munich, Germany.

RIGHT **1932:** A little boy plays St George with a Komodo dragon at London Zoo, England.

1972: Children pedal a tricycle constructed from discarded bric-a-brac and household goods. Location not known.

1972: A second improvized vehicle utilizes a pram as a base and a megaphone for communication. Location not known.

1938: Children look excitedly at the snow from a window in a National Adoption home, England.

RIGHT **c. 1928:** Children seated in a shop window in London, England.

1955: An International Brotherhood of Magicians meeting in Lancashire, England.

RIGHT **c. 1910:** An acrobatic father-and-son team.

1965: Seven-year-old Jeanette Lewis playing with a six-foot-tall Trimline telephone made by the Western Electric Company to display at company locations.

RIGHT **c. 1940:** A little girl sitting in a giant ski-shoe made by a Viennese shoemaker.

1942: Fifteen-month-old Rodney Twitchett peers out from his hiding place in an upturned suitcase, England.

c. 1930: Twins in a suitcase in Austria.

1944: Children with a push-chair camouflaged by leaves and branches during the liberation of Paris in August.

c. 1900: A baby perched in a leafy bush next to the porch of a Victorian house in America.

LEFT **1990s:** Two young boys in animal-like iron masks clutching swords at the Big Green Gathering, England.

1951: A girl wearing a giraffe head by the designer Charles Eames.

1925: A little girl in a striped suit at a zoo in Germany.

1939: A young girl takes a closer look at a hooded bird of prey, England.

1961: Timothy Pratt inspects the engine of his toy car. Location not known.

RIGHT **1952:** Children give a full service to a large wooden car. Location not known.

1954: An angry man waves his fist at a group of mischief makers during Leeds Mischief Night, England.

1925: A young boy attaches a firework to a policeman. Location not known.

LEFT **c. 1960s:** A group of children queuing for petrol at a toy garage in Middlesex, England.

1934: A man out walking his dog points out a "No Parking" sign to a young girl who has stopped her toy car beside it. Location not known.

1938: Two costumed young women are offered a ride by a young man. Location not known.

c. 1920s: A group of young girls pose on a sidewalk. Location not known.

1951: Pauline Darley holds her doll and a python called Rajah in the courtyard of her London home.

1950s: A baby plays with a snake. Location not known.

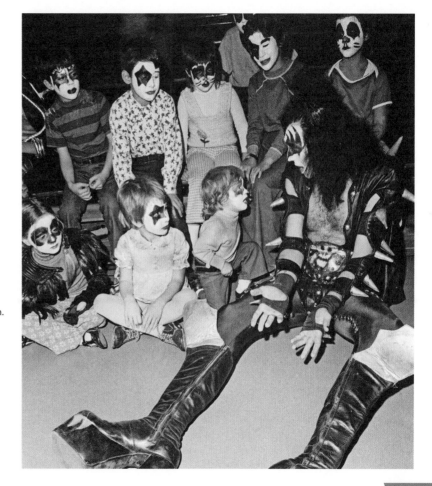

LEFT **c. 1966:**
American actor
Adam West,
as Batman in
Kensington, London.

1975: Gene
Simmons of the
rock-and-roll band
"KISS" makes
some new friends
before performing
at Cadillac
High School's
homecoming,
Michigan, USA.

c.1860: A juvenile hypnotist places a young girl (and her doll) in a trance, France.

1911: Two girls feed each other by blindfold. Location not known.

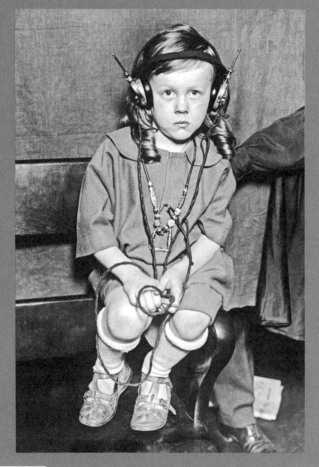

c. 1925: A young
girl listens to
a crystal radio.
Location not known.

RIGHT **1925:** A little
girl is delighted by a
valve radio. Location
not known.

1955: A rally in Trinidad Park for the arrival of Princess Margaret in Trinidad and Tobago.

RIGHT **1920s:** Two boys recline in Willamette's huge meteorite found in Oregon, USA.

WILLAMETTE

1946: Babies crawling toward a mobile row of stuffed rabbits during the 8th annual Diaper Service Derby. Location not known.

1956: A small child plays with a big rabbit at a shopping mall Easter Wonderland. Location not known.

1973: A schoolboy reads a comic, Sussex, England.

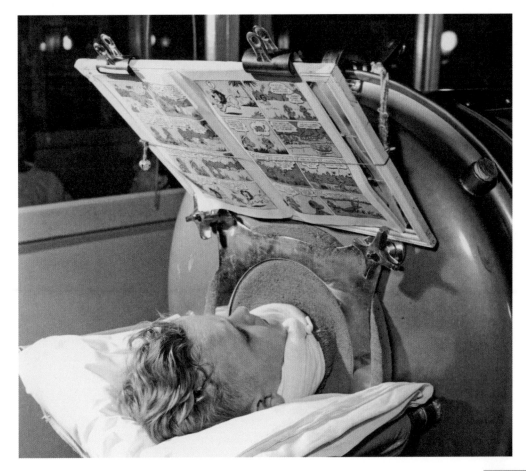

1955: A child reads a comic while in an iron lung. Location not known.

1941: A boy rides a catfish in Texas, USA.

1959: A boy and girl with "Master Ichiro," a two-meter-tall humanoid robot designed to walk and to speak by means of microphones in its head. Location not known.

1965: A boy operates a remote-controlled robot. Location not known.

1937: A mother fastens a notice onto her son's back before he sets out on a trial bicycle ride. Location not known.

1957: Three young dancers outside a dance hall. Location not known.

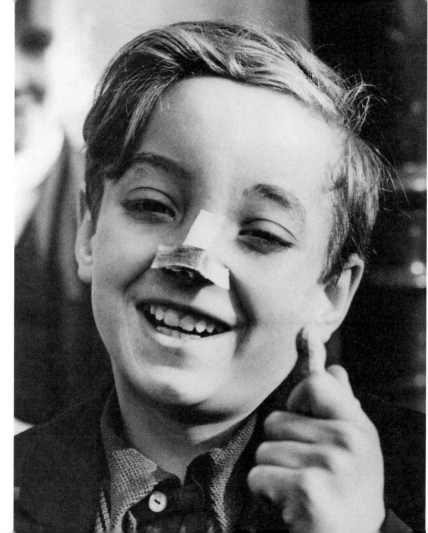

LEFT **1938:**
Children in King's
Cross Street,
London, push
peanuts along
the pavement with
their noses in a
race to cross the
finishing line.

1938: A participant
holds up his winning
peanut, King's Cross
Street, London.

1939: A boy surveys his miniature army. Location not known.

1940: Children playing with hundreds of military soldier figurines. Location not known.

c. 1920: A boy smokes a fat cigar. Location not known.

1928: Two young boys play at "smoking." Location not known.

c. 1920s: A young girl lights a cigarette from a match box. Location not known.

RIGHT **c. 1900:** Young strawberry pickers in Hampshire, England, smoking cigarettes during a well-earned break.

1941: Two little girls reading a board advertising carrots instead of ice lollies, a result of wartime shortages of ice cream. Location not known.

1965: Mr Ernest Castro's ventriloquist doll "Lettice Leefe." Location not known.

1955: Three-year-old twins Maureen and Leigh Soden play with a three-foot-high toy astronaut doll at the American Rocket Society scientific exhibit.

1955: A spaceman's outfit produced at a toy factory in Palmers Green, London. The walkie-talkie set works over a distance of 600 yards.

1973: In Hungary, children playing on a playground's "Aquarius" lunar landing unit on a housing estate.

RIGHT **1950:** A girl plays with a Moonwalker. The robot was intended to imitate the walking of astronauts on the moon. Location not known.

1976: Eight-year-old Mark Harman from London enjoying a game of Monopoly with his brother Graham and sister Belinda. Mark spent two hours every other evening relaxing on his nail bed.

1977: A boy loses his balance in a skateboard race against a pot plant. Location not known.

LEFT 1999: Children play in small tanks on an ice rink on the frozen Songhua River, China.

1946: Children playing with a mock tank at an adventure playground in Copenhagen, Denmark.

1973: Six-year-old Adam Blanchard plays a thoughtful game of chess with Tommy, a 10-year-old Capuchin monkey from South America. Location not known.

1953: A baby elephant from Assam at the Children's Zoo, Regents Park, London pulling a child along.

1975: Barry Lapworth of Hastings, England, cycles on a miniature bike along the seafront.

1928: Child cast members, riding in their unusual homemade car, in a promotional still for the "Our Gang" film "Edison, Marconi & Co." Location not known.

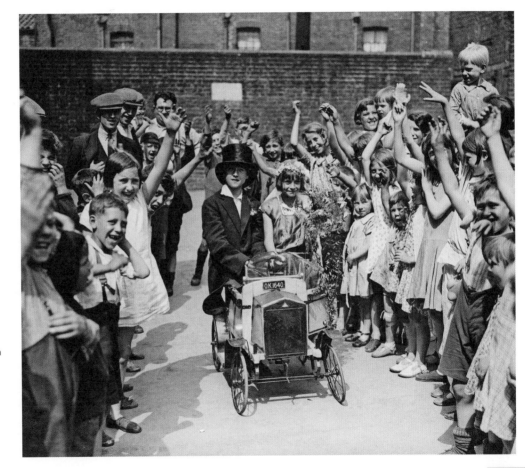

LEFT **1952:** A May Day festival "wedding" between two children.

1932: Children in the slum streets of Caledonian Road, London play at "getting married."

LEFT **1922:** A boy with a kite made of banknotes in Germany.

1923: Children using notes of money as building blocks during the German inflation crisis.

1943: A day nursery in the East End of London, where the children shelter in a linen cupboard during an air raid.

1964: A woman and child at a London dog show.

THAT'S ALL FOLKS!

ACKNOWLEDGMENTS

Thank you to Zara Larcombe, Natalia Price-Cabrera, Tina Smith, Roly Allen, and Andrew Gordon. Thank you also to Alex Q. Arbuckle, Stephanie Buck, Pete Cashmore, Dustin Drankoski, Mike Kriak, Adam Ostrow, Chris Phillips, Jim Roberts, Christoph Shcholz, and Darren Tome. Special thanks to digital curator Amanda Uren.

PICTURE CREDITS